Whispers of the Woodland

In the thicket, squirrels dance,
Chasing shadows like a trance.
An owl wears glasses, quite absurd,
It reads the news, or so I've heard.

A rabbit plays the ukulele,
While foxes juggle berries daily.
The raccoons have a comedy show,
With jokes that make the wild things glow.

Original title:
A Forest of Fables

Copyright © 2025 Creative Arts Management OÜ
All rights reserved.

Author: Julian Montgomery
ISBN HARDBACK: 978-1-80567-410-8
ISBN PAPERBACK: 978-1-80567-709-3

Tales Beneath the Canopy

Beneath the leaves, the stories lie,
Where frogs recite their haiku high.
A bear who swears he's quite the chef,
Serves salad made from stolen treble clef.

The badger's plan was sheer delight,
To throw a party every night.
With dancing ants and beetles brave,
They rock the woodlands like a rave.

The Enchanted Glade

In glades where twinkling fairies play,
A grumpy troll sighs, "Where's my pay?"
He runs a toll booth by the stream,
Collecting coins for every dream.

A butterfly stirs up some gossip,
Spreading tales of a frog who's a prophet.
Wicked weasels weave their schemes,
While singing birds just burst with memes.

Secrets in the Shade

The shadows hold a jester's grin,
Who tells of squirrels' silly wins.
A hedgehog gets a hairdo bright,
Confident, he struts in the light.

A mouse with dreams of fame and flair,
Wants to launch his line of underwear.
While trees reach out, they stretch and yawn,
As laughter spills with each new dawn.

Dreamswoven in the Dew

When the sun spills gold on the grass,
A squirrel wears shades, in style, with sass.
The rabbits dance to a tune quite absurd,
While the wise old owl just spreads the word.

A mouse in a coat sips tea from a nut,
Telling tall tales from a soft little hut.
The breeze whispers jokes to the flowers arrayed,
As giggles erupt in the dew-lightened glade.

Spirits of the Hidden Dell

In a dell where secrets frequently meet,
The frogs wear top hats, quite dapper and neat.
The crickets recite poetry polished and bright,
While fireflies twinkle like stars in the night.

A tortoise raps with a beat of his shell,
Bringing laughter so loud it rings like a bell.
With a tap dance from hedgehogs, the fun's never done,
As raccoons juggle berries for everyone's fun.

The Unity of the Wild Ones

A gathering sparked where the wild ones unite,
With laughter that ripples like rays of soft light.
The deer tell tall tales of leaps that they've made,
While foxes perform mime in a cool forest shade.

Squirrels collect treasures from branches above,
As badgers play poker, all suited with love.
Amongst the tall grasses, their merry song swells,
In roles that they play, 'tis a world full of spells.

Fantasies of Fern and Frond

With ferns as their hats, the critters parade,
Each twist of a leaf, a new role they've displayed.
A hedgehog holds court, with a crown made of moss,
While dancing ants march, they've made quite the toss.

In the wild wonder of whispers and glee,
The beetles recite lines of old poetry.
With giggles and quirks, the day breezes on,
Each fantasy woven till dusk greets the dawn.

Nature's Narrative: A Tapestry of Tales

Once a squirrel wore a tiny hat,
He'd scurry about, thinking he was fat.
Chasing shadows while munching nuts,
Claiming the crown of the forest's ruts.

An owl with glasses read every page,
Laughing at rabbits claiming the stage.
A hedgehog poet recited his verse,
While ants held a dance that turned quite diverse.

Myths Among the Maple Trees

A bear tried ballet, oh what a sight,
Twirling with grace in the soft moonlight.
But tripped on a root, fell flat on the floor,
Yet laughed with the trees, wanting more and more.

Fox told tall tales of his stealthy stunts,
But fell in a puddle and laughed, "Aren't I blunt?"
The chipmunks chuckled, holding their sides,
While squirrels debated who takes the prize.

The Quest of the Quiet Quagmire

In a quagmire lived a chatty old frog,
Claiming to have danced with a clever old dog.
His stories stretched far, quite humorous too,
As he croaked 'bout adventures of things he once knew.

A snail armed with dreams took his time with each step,
Challenging breezes, though full of inept.
Behind him, a worm made a hilarious mess,
Fumble and tumble, yet thriving nonetheless.

Spirits in the Serene Grove

Ghosts in the grove played hide and seek,
Shuffling and laughing, oh what a peek!
One tripped on a root and let out a squeal,
The trees all giggled, what a surreal deal!

A mischievous spirit threw pinecones with glee,
While shadows danced wildly, forever carefree.
They told tales of laughter that echoed so bright,
In a grove full of giggles, all through the night.

Legends Lurking in the Leaffall

In the rustle of leaves, a tale is spun,
A squirrel in a cape, oh what a run!
He chases his acorns, they laugh and flee,
Dancing like nuts, up high in the tree.

A raccoon with glasses, reading a map,
Claims he's the king, invincible chap.
His crown made of twigs, a sight to behold,
He prances so proudly, so foolish and bold.

A fox paints his whiskers in colors so bright,
Telling the trees that he's a bird in flight.
They chuckle and sway, in the soft, gentle breeze,
While he fluffs his tail, trying hard to please.

But whispers of legends still swirl in the air,
Of creatures and mischief and wild woodland dare.
In this leafy kingdom, laughter is found,
Among the old trees, stories abound.

Parables of the Peeking Sun

The sun peeks through branches, a cheeky glow,
A rabbit in shades says, 'Hey, don't be slow!'
He's sizzling up carrots, in a frying pan,
Telling the world he's a gourmet man.

A wise old owl, with a hat of three sizes,
Keeps falling asleep, filled with silly surprises.
Whenever he snores, the leaves start to shake,
And all of his dreams make the forest awake.

The butterflies giggle, flitting about,
They wear tiny boots, oh, without a doubt!
Teaching the bees some dance moves to share,
"Oh buzz like a pro, if you dare, if you dare!"

Every branch has a tale, and every tree grins,
With laughter entwined, where the sunlight begins.
In this whimsical world, where giggles abound,
The parables bloom, in laughter, they're crowned.

Secrets of the Sylvan Solstice

On the day of the solstice, the shadows all play,
A hedgehog in pajamas claims, 'This is my day!'
He rolls down a hill, then leaps in the air,
A tumble of laughter, quite the furry affair.

A badger who juggles with nuts and some rocks,
Declares he's amazing, the king of the blocks.
But as he goes wild, one slip, and oh no!
The audience roars, as he faces the woe.

A deer with a horn made of glitter and glue,
Sings silly ballads that ring ever true.
All critters unite in a clamor of cheer,
As twilight arrives, filling hearts with good cheer.

And as the stars twinkle in nighttime's embrace,
The silly ol' stories find their own place.
Secrets entwined in each leaf, every sound,
In this jubilant wood, where joy can be found.

The Ballad of the Blossoming Bough

A bough that was bare, now bursting with blooms,
A frog in a top hat, declares, "Here's the room!"
He hosts a grand dance with insects in style,
All twirling together, oh, isn't it vile?

The bees come in flocks for the sweetest of treats,
With honey on toast, oh, the fun never beats.
They buzz and they bop, like they own all the space,
While fireflies twinkle, adding flair to the place.

A chipmunk recites a poem of sass,
About acorns and laughter, oh, that little rascal mass!
He boasts of adventures he hasn't, of course,
While the trees shake their branches, with laughter's own force.

In this playful glade, where whimsy takes flight,
Every creature finds joy in the soft, gentle light.
The ballad shall linger, in echoes of cheer,
As the blossoms keep blooming, year after year.

Tales Beneath the Old Oak

Once a squirrel, quite spry and bold,
Found a nut that glittered like gold.
He claimed it a treasure, oh what a sight,
But it rolled off and gave him a fright.

A rabbit with glasses, so wise and keen,
Wrote a book on the grass, oh what a scene!
But the wind blew hard, and the pages flew,
He chased them down, what else could he do?

The hedgehog danced in a tutu bright,
While chipmunks snapped selfies, pure delight.
They laughed and twirled under the sun,
In this silly world, they had such fun.

At dusk, an owl shared tales at the end,
Of a rooster who thought he could ascend.
With each silly story, giggles would swell,
In this cheerful grove, all was well!

The Secrets of Sylvan Shadows

In the shade where whispers dwell,
A jittery fox with stories to tell.
He convinced a crow to trade him a snack,
For a tale of a wolf who played the flute in black.

A turtle once raced a swift morning breeze,
Thinking he'd win with incredible ease.
He tripped on a root, went head over heels,
And landed right smack where the mushroom peels.

A band of mice formed a rock band grand,
With tiny guitars made from twigs in hand.
Their concert was loud, but also quite squeaky,
They serenaded the trees, it was rather cheeky.

The shadows giggled as the night grew long,
With creatures dancing to their own silly song.
In this world of wonder, laughter ran free,
Secrets danced lightly, just like the glee.

Enchanted Glades and Gossamer Dreams

In a glade where silly wishes bloom,
A moose wore a hat with a feather plume.
He strutted around like he owned the place,
While frogs cheered him on in a wacky race.

A gnome with a penchant for magic tricks,
Pulled rabbits from hats with some frantic flicks.
But one jumped right out and stole his shoe,
Leaving the gnome hopping, what else to do?

An owl on a swing sang high in the trees,
Trading wise quips with the buzzing bees.
They freestyled together beneath the full moon,
In this jovial world, where laughter's in tune.

As stars twinkled down on this whimsical realm,
Creatures all gathered, taking the helm.
With giggles and tales shared over the stream,
Every heart fluttered, alive with a dream.

Sagas of the Starlit Grove

In the starlit grove, where the grass glows bright,
A cat wore pajamas, what a funny sight!
He strutted about, proud of his flair,
While a hedgehog took selfies, unaware.

A brood of wild geese held a debate,
On who can be the absolute great.
They squawked and flapped, what a chaotic scene,
While the wise old turtle just sipped his green.

A beaver chewed on a log with flair,
Dreaming of castles built in midair.
But when he bit down, the log gave a crack,
And he found himself stuck, with no way back!

And as moonbeams played with the rustling leaves,
The creatures all giggled, just like old thieves.
In the starlit grove, where stories take flight,
Laughter echoed loud, a wonderful night.

Legends of the Leafy Haven

In the shade where chatter grew,
A squirrel wore a hat of blue.
He boasted of his acorn stash,
But tripped and made a comical crash.

The wise old owl gave a wink,
As branches swayed with a gentle clink.
A rabbit danced in fancy shoes,
While crickets played the funniest blues.

Beneath the sun, the vines would swing,
And flowers joined the silly fling.
They told of tales where laughter reigned,
In this haven where fun remained.

So gather 'round, both young and old,
For stories here are bright and bold.
With giggles that will never cease,
In leafy realms of endless peace.

The Song of the Timber Spirits

In whispers soft, the spirits sing,
Their melody is quite the thing.
An acorn slipped from mighty oak,
And giggled hard at all the smoke.

The pine trees swayed with chilly grace,
As squirrels raced in a wild chase.
A log became a dancing floor,
With critters clapping, wanting more!

Laughter echoed through the glade,
As every shade of green displayed.
The bees would buzz in tuned delight,
As sunlight turned the day to night.

In moonlit beams, the tales were spun,
Of timber spirits having fun.
So when you hear their joyful choir,
Know life's a dance in leafy fire.

Fables Written in Bark

Underneath the crooked tree,
A tale was carved so skillfully.
A bear wore shades and rode a bike,
While squirrels cheered with all their might.

The raccoon slipped on banana peels,
Creating all the funniest squeals.
A goat played chess with a wise old fox,
As mushrooms grew like silly socks.

Those fables told in nature's ink,
Make even grumpy toads rethink.
For every swipe of bark and brush,
Hides laughter in a joyful hush.

So read the signs that nature gives,
Where playful thoughts and humor lives.
Each tale a twist, a laugh, a spark,
In this enchanted, vibrant park.

The Mystique of the Evergreen

Beneath the boughs of emerald green,
Lived critters who were rarely seen.
A hedgehog wore a tiny crown,
While gnomes put on a show in town.

The trees would sway, a happy dance,
With flickering lights that made you prance.
A woodpecker drummed a silly beat,
As rabbits brought in snacks to eat.

With tales of giants made of bark,
And frogs who croaked 'til quite dark.
The air was filled with giggles bright,
In this woodland full of pure delight.

So wander near the green-clad trails,
Where humor lives and joy prevails.
For in this realm of curious schemes,
You'll find the magic of your dreams.

The Chronicles of Secret Sprouts

In the garden, beans took flight,
They danced under the moonlight.
Radishes held a debate,
While carrots plotted their great fate.

Broccoli wore a crown so bright,
As peppers juggled, a comical sight.
Cucumbers tried their best to rhyme,
All in a row, keeping perfect time.

The tomatoes, red with glee,
Cheered on the dancing parsley.
As lettuce laughed, it slipped and fell,
Creating chaos, oh what a yell!

In this realm of sprout delight,
Every veggie's a star tonight.
Their stories, wild and sweet,
A mischievous garden, where friends meet.

Fables Found on Fern Fronds

Once a squirrel with tales to tell,
Sipped tea with a wise old shell.
A joke was cracked, the mossy floor,
Giggled softly, wanting more.

A raccoon wore a fancy hat,
Declared himself the king of chat.
With tales of theft and gourmet trash,
He entertained with style and flash.

The ferns danced with a fluttering cheer,
As bunnies gathered all near.
They spun stories, round and round,
Until their laughter filled the ground.

From every leaf, a secret sprung,
In every crevice, funny songs sung.
A world where whimsy freely flows,
On ferny fronds, where hilarity grows.

Memoirs from the Mysterious Moss

In the hush of twilight's sway,
Moss critters gathered 'round to play.
A snail told tales of a daring race,
While mushrooms giggled with a rosy face.

A hedgehog danced with tiny feet,
Crafting rhymes that couldn't be beat.
With thorns for pens and dew for ink,
They chronicled dreams and made us think.

A worm poked through, with witty glee,
Declared, "This world's a comedy!"
With puns and jests, they shared their find,
In the cozy embrace, laughter was kind.

In that mossy realm, with giggles bright,
Every creature felt just right.
These memoirs, a riotous fuzzy tome,
In the soft, green carpet, they called home.

Reflections of the Rooted Realms

In the depths where the roots reside,
Tales of splendor often hide.
A wise old tree shared a hearty laugh,
As bugs played cards, enjoying their craft.

A beetle bragged of journeys vast,
Claimed he'd seen the very last.
While crickets chirped, their rhythm grand,
Creating music across the land.

A twirling leaf caught everyone's eye,
As it spun like a dervish in the sky.
The ground erupted in joyous applause,
For the quirky antics of nature's laws.

These rooted realms of whimsy and cheer,
Echo stories we all hold dear.
In every quirk, a laughter streams,
Life's a cycle of playful dreams.

Lullabies of the Leafy Abyss

In a nook where the owls play,
Squirrels dance on a branch all day.
A fox with a hat sings a tune,
While raccoons jiggle under the moon.

A rabbit with glasses reads a tale,
Of brave bugs that sail on a snail.
They giggle at shadows that prance,
And join in a whimsical dance.

The leaves rustle soft, like a sigh,
As the butterflies flutter and fly.
An ant with a drum keeps the beat,
While grasshoppers tap dancing feet.

So snuggle in tight under this tree,
Where laughter blooms wild and carefree.
In the depths of the magical dark,
Each creature holds dreams with a spark.

The Heartbeat of Hidden Hollow

Where the wind whispers secrets unknown,
A turtle with sunglasses lingers alone.
He chats with a snail about the weather,
Sharing stories, they lighten the tether.

A bear in pajamas takes a stroll,
Searching for honey to fill up his bowl.
He trips on a root but gives a loud laugh,
And ends in a puddle, oh what a gaffe!

The crickets compose in the lovely dusk,
While fireflies twinkle—a sight to trust.
They share silly dances, a comedic flick,
And the night giggles at every trick.

So if you should wander this curious land,
With chuckles and grins, you'll find it is grand.
Each shadow and smile, a jest on the way,
Welcome to mirth where all creatures play.

Verses from the Verdant Veil

Under the shade of a giant pine,
A raccoon is cooking a meal with a twine.
The chattering birds offer spices from flight,
Creating a feast, oh what a delight!

A frog hops in wearing bright polka dots,
Declaring his love for the curviest pots.
His friends all gather, eyebrows all raised,
As he shows off his dish, looking quite fazed.

Beneath a bouquet of fluttering leaves,
They share funny jokes that nobody believes.
With giggles and snorts, the laughter ignites,
In this charming place, all feel so light.

So join in their fun through valleys and glades,
Each critter a gem, in bright masquerades.
In the depths of this tale, joy is on sale,
In a place where the whimsical never goes stale.

Fables of the Flickering Fireflies

At dusk when the glowworms begin to blink,
A squirrel concocts a wild drink.
With acorns and berries, he shakes up a shake,
Becoming the talk of the woodland lake.

The fireflies giggle, twinkling with flair,
Chasing each other through fragrant air.
A ladybug winks as she flies on by,
Saying, "Join the fun, let's light up the sky!"

A hedgehog plays music on leaves that he found,
While crickets keep rhythm with their joyful sound.
In this garden of laughter that never gets old,
Even the tiniest beetles feel bold.

So when the sun sets and stars fill the space,
Remember this place, full of joy and grace.
Each flicker and flutter, a merry parade,
In the tales where laughter and magic are made.

Stories Woven in the Branches

In a realm where squirrels chat,
And owls wear hats, oh how they sat!
The rabbits tell tales of their grand race,
While the tortoise rolls, just keeping pace.

A fox with a flair, so slick and sly,
Claims he can dance, oh my, oh my!
With squirrels and birds tapping their toes,
The hedgehog sneezes, and away it goes.

The bees buzz songs about sweet honey,
While a lazy bear laughs, oh it's so funny!
The trees clap along, with leaves that shake,
As the groundhogs giggle, for goodness' sake!

With every turn, more antics rise,
Gnomes pull pranks under sunny skies.
In this tangled realm, joy spins like a fate,
A merry tale, filled with laughs, how great!

The Odyssey of the Overgrown Path

A path less traveled, where mischief thrives,
With snails on scooters and giggly gripes.
A weasel, charmed, plays tricks all day,
While hedgehogs wonder, "Is that a play?"

Frogs leap high with croaky cheer,
Spinning tales of adventures near.
The path is twisted with giggles and sighs,
As fireflies dance under moonlit skies.

A clumsy moose trips on a log,
And giggles as he chases a fog.
The mushrooms laugh as they sway and bend,
In this wacky world, where humor won't end.

Around each corner, a surprise awaits,
Laughter echoes through the garden gates.
With every step on the playful track,
The heart grows lighter, no looking back!

Fables in the Ferns

Among the ferns, whispers abound,
Where odd critters waddle all around.
A parrot tells jokes with comedic flair,
While the hedgehogs giggle, without a care.

With stories shared at the foot of a tree,
A spider dreams of webs so free.
She spins a yarn that tickles the air,
Making all creatures stop, look, and stare.

The frogs debate if they can sing,
While a lizard practices his bling.
The crickets chirp in rhythmic beats,
As laughter flows with the warm scents of sweets.

Through dappled light, the fun persists,
With fables written on the morning mist.
In this lively world of ferny delights,
Each nook and cranny welcomes funny sights.

Echoes of the Elders

Wise old owls with stories to share,
Perch on branches, send laughter in the air.
They recount the days of yore and glee,
When shadows danced and troubles were free.

A rabbit recounts his wild escape,
From clumsy cats dressed in capes.
The raccoons chime in with a raucous cheer,
As the elder tree shakes, drawing them near.

Beneath the moon, the laughter swells,
Each creature with stories, how freely it dwells.
Bathed in twilight, their giggles inspire,
As echoes of past, like shadows, conspire.

And so they gather, both young and old,
To hear the tales, and let them unfold.
In this grove where joy never fades,
The echoes of laughter become leafy parades.

Whims of the Wildwood

In the trees a squirrel leapt,
He tripped on roots and squeaked,
A rabbit laughed until he wept,
While nearby, owls just peeked.

A raccoon donned a silly hat,
Declared himself the king,
The frogs began to dance and chat,
As crickets started to sing.

The deer wore socks of vibrant pink,
While foxes played a game,
They all paused for a drink,
At the stream—oh what a fame!

Each creature had a silly tale,
Of jokes that filled the air,
In the woods where chuckles sail,
Fun lived everywhere!

Epistles of the Echoing Embers

A firefly wrote a letter clear,
Beware the shadow of a hare,
It hops so high, it'll cause a cheer,
And land you flat without a care!

The mushrooms held a meeting bright,
To discuss how ants would march,
They giggled at their silly sights,
Each bump and wiggle set to parge.

A bear wearing glasses read with glee,
Of ants that danced in a parade,
"Oh what a sight, how could that be?"
They all applauded, quite afraid!

So gather round, dear woodland friends,
And hear these tales of joy,
For laughter is a blend that bends,
Even spirits young and coy!

Tales of the Timeless Thicket

In the thicket where shadows play,
A hedgehog rolled into a tree,
He spun around in such a way,
That all the critters danced in spree.

The turtles tried to race so fast,
But slipped on mud and went askew,
They splashed and giggled as they passed,
While geese honked loud, "Oh, what's new?"

A wise old fox began to joke,
He told a tale of clumsy bears,
Who wore their shoes made out of oak,
And slipped right off their furry lairs!

Each creature danced till night was nigh,
Stars blinked down with twinkling eyes,
In the thicket, oh my oh my,
Laughter weaved the evening skies!

Musings from the Moonlit Glade

By the moonlit brook, a chipmunk danced,
He twirled with glee, lost in the sound,
A turtle sighed, "Give me a chance,"
But all his feet just whirled around.

Two owls played chess 'neath the bright stars,
With acorns piled high as stakes,
One hooted, "I'll bet you my car!"
And laughed as the other one shakes.

A porcupine dressed up as a knight,
With sticks and feathers in his gear,
Around the fire, they laughed till bright,
Each story nixed all trace of fear!

In the glade, joy stitched the night air,
As critters shared their silly jests,
With every laugh, they spawned a rare,
Bond of friendship, that surely rests!

Fables From the Ferny Underworld

In the thicket where the hedgehogs snore,
Bats play poker, always wanting more.
Mice gossip over cheese and bread,
While frogs do ballet, earning space to tread.

The owls hoot with wisdom perplexed,
Claiming they're still pondering their next text.
Meanwhile, squirrels throw acorn parties bright,
As snails arrive, slow yet full of delight.

Tales unfold where odd critters meet,
Raccoons dance in shoes far too neat.
Chasing fireflies, giggles abound,
In this wild world, pure joy is found.

When dawn breaks, laughter rings like a bell,
In this ferny underworld, all is well.
With each fable spun from leafy dreams,
Nature's comedy flows in vibrant streams.

The Enigma of the Emerald Realm

In the glow of greens where secrets creep,
Leprechauns sneak in, not a peep.
They trade shiny buttons for a jig,
While dancing worms show off a big gig.

A gopher schemes on who'll win the race,
While rabbits hop with a grin on their face.
Owls try hard not to snore at the show,
As wise old turtles just take it slow.

Chasing shadows, the shadows then chase,
A raccoon finds nuts but leaves without grace.
In emerald leaves, mischief's in the air,
With every rustle, a fanciful dare.

Each night unveils a brand-new delight,
As critters frolic under the moonlight.
In this emerald realm, laughter's the theme,
Where nothing is ever quite as it seems.

Parables of Pine and Moss

On the carpet of pine where the ants parade,
A wise old crow gives advice unmade.
"Gather your snacks, but mind your hat,"
Said the sneaky raccoon in his jovial chat.

Mossy tales drift on breezes' breath,
Where tales of the past flirt with death.
A fox brings punch, and the deer love to sip,
While beetles form chains for their grand funny trip.

The roots below hum ancient lore,
As butterflies giggle, wanting more.
With every branch that sways in glee,
Comes a whisper of mischief, wild and free.

In the shadows where the shrooms grow tall,
Funny stories echo and call.
Underneath the moss, hidden delight,
Parables arise in the soft twilight.

Shadows of the Silent Glade

In shadows thick, where whispers dwell,
A chattering chipmunk sings a funny spell.
Mushrooms wear hats like stars on parade,
While beetles stomp to the music they've made.

A mysterious owl tries to play chess,
But nobody comes, oh what a mess!
The frogs on the lily pads start to cheer,
With smiles so wide, it's hard not to leer.

Wily foxes play pranks, oh what a sight,
Swapping their tails just for pure delight.
In this silent glade, giggles abound,
As laughter erupts from the earth's very ground.

With each tale spun in the shade of the trees,
The shadows share laughter caught on the breeze.
In the heart of the glade, beneath the night's glow,
The funny fables of nature bestow.

Myths of the Moonlit Meadow

In shadows deep, where critters play,
A rabbit claims it's here to stay.
It dances bright, with quite a flair,
But trips on roots, flies through the air.

A wise old owl, with glasses thick,
Tells jokes that land with quite a kick.
The stars above begin to chuckle,
As giggling sprites begin to buckle.

The fireflies glow, a twinkling sight,
They stumble 'round, from left to right.
They think they're stars, doing their best,
Until they land, in blooms, and rest.

So gather round, embrace the cheer,
The meadow's tales, they all hold dear.
In laughter's light, we spin our dreams,
In moonlit glee, we burst at seams.

Ballads Beneath the Bark

Beneath the bark, a raccoon sings,
With pots and pans, he makes them ring.
A band of squirrels joins the beat,
They dance to rhythms, oh so sweet!

A turtle claims he'll steal the show,
In boots too big, he steals the glow.
But gliding past, he takes a tumble,
And all the forest starts to rumble!

A badger holds a microphone,
And tells a tale that's all his own.
He spins a yarn, the crowd's in stitches,
About the day when he found riches!

Laughter roots us, binds with charm,
In this wild glade, it's safe from harm.
With every note that fills the air,
We find our joy, our hearts laid bare.

The Chronicles of the Canopied Realm

In branches high, a squirrel dreams,
Of acorns bigger than moonbeams.
He plans a feast, a grand display,
But birds swoop in, and fly away!

An old tree stump holds whispers tight,
Of secret feasts and silly fights.
The gnomes parade with tiny hats,
While dodging giggling, taunting rats!

The breeze joins in, a chuckling breeze,
As everyone laughs and none feels uneasy.
While lily pads join the scene,
Tomorrow's snack might be quite the glean!

So tales unfold, beneath the sky,
With snickering leaves that wave goodbye.
In canopies where dreams take flight,
We celebrate with sheer delight.

Whispers of Old Woodland Wishes

The whispering pines, they tell a joke,
Of a bear who thought he could smoke.
He lit a twig, oh what a sight,
The flames were bright, but he took flight!

A hedgehog joins with quills on show,
He dreams of being quite a pro.
But when he rolls, he bumps a tree,
And ends up dizzy, oh so free!

The mushrooms giggle in a patch,
As frogs declare a warty match.
They leap and bound with potbelly pride,
While all the crickets cheer and hide!

In woodland hazes, laughter sings,
Echoing through the air, it rings.
For in this place of timeless lore,
We share our dreams, forevermore.

Insights of the Illuminated Isle

On this isle, where shadows prance,
A chicken learned to play a dance.
With feet so light and heart so bold,
He twirled on dreams, a sight to behold.

The fish wore hats, quite gay and bright,
They held a party every night.
With jellybeans and dancing snails,
They laughed and sang, the fish told tales.

A wise old owl, with glasses on,
Scribbled notes till the break of dawn.
He'd snicker low, 'What can they think?'
As squirrels pondered with drinks of pink.

In light of day, they all would play,
In their own funny, quirky way.
Each creature living with drink and cheer,
In this isle where laughter's ever near.

The Spirit of the Sturdy Saplings

In a grove where giggles bloom,
A tree told jokes to chase the gloom.
With branches swaying like a clown,
It made the butterflies fall down.

A mischievous raccoon, quite spry,
Swapped all the nuts for pink pie.
The squirrels squeaked in great dismay,
'What's this? We wanted snacks today!'

A log would roll and laugh so loud,
While snails brought in a silly crowd.
With party hats and tiny drinks,
They danced, they twirled, they winked in sync.

The hoots and chirps echoed the tale,
Of saplings with spirits that would not fail.
In this nook, under pure delight,
The spirits soared, all day and night.

Fables Nestled in Nectar

In the blossoms, sweetness flows,
Buzzing bees wear tiny clothes.
They hold a race around the bloom,
While ants dance out, dispelling gloom.

A butterfly, dressed up in style,
Decided it would run a mile.
With petals bright and stripes to show,
It wiggled left, it wiggled slow.

Beetles played tag beneath the sun,
And snickered loud, "This is just fun!"
A ladybug cheered them all along,
Singing sweetly a silly song.

With nectar sweet and laughter near,
These tales unfold, bringing cheer.
In petals soft, and sunshine warm,
Nestled are fables, a merry swarm.

Tales Under the Twilight Canopy

Beneath the boughs, where shadows grow,
A tiny mouse put on a show.
With cheese as props and laughs galore,
He stole the night with every roar.

Fireflies blinked, like stars in flight,
Forming lines, their dance a sight.
They wiggled with glee, excitedly,
As frogs played tunes on lily leaves.

A wise old bat hung upside down,
Chortling with glee, wearing a crown.
"Join me, friends! Let's spin a tale,
Of silly naps and spicy snails!"

Under twilight's soft embrace,
Laughter flows in this playful space.
With stories shared and spirits free,
These fables weave in harmony.

The Timeless Tangle of Tales

In a land where the trees wear hats,
A squirrel sings songs about acrobats.
He twirls on branches, a daring feat,
While the owls hoot tunes for a lively beat.

A rabbit jogs by with a tiny drum,
Playing a rhythm, oh so fun!
The hedgehog comments from a nearby stone,
"Rhythms and rhymes, here we call home!"

The frogs form a band on a lilypad grand,
Plucking at strings with their sticky hands.
They croak a chorus, loud and bright,
While the fireflies dance, in sheer delight.

Under twinkling stars in a jolly row,
The stories unfold, and the laughter will flow.
In this land of giggles, adventure prevails,
As the whispers of joy weave through fantastical tales.

Harmonies of the Verdant Hideaway

In a glade where the daisies wear bright bows,
A shy little mouse strikes a pose that glows.
He twirled around, not a care in his heart,
With a tune in the air, oh, he plays the part!

The badger joins in with a raucous laugh,
Chasing a butterfly, caught in a gaffe.
He trips on a root, tumbling down,
And soon the whole glade resembles a clown town!

A pair of raccoons hold a cake-decorating spree,
With frosting on noses, and giggles, oh me!
They craft a delight that the skunks love to eat,
While the whole woodland joins in, snacking sweet!

Beneath a sky that echoes with glee,
A leafy cabaret, joyous and free.
Here, laughter and stories blend with the moon,
In a land where the melodies dance to a tune.

Whispers of the Woodland

When the sunbeams wink through the canopy bright,
The chipmunks tell tales, igniting delight.
With a wiggle and jiggle, they're prancing about,
Sharing secrets, with squeaks and with shouts.

A wise old tree with a gnarled, crooked grin,
Holds the key to the tales locked deep from within.
"With a splash of humor and a sprinkle of cheer,
Let's laugh till our roots tangle near!"

The rabbits in costumes of polka dot flair,
Host a party while twirling in midair.
With hats made of leaves and shoes of fine moss,
They dance in a circle, without a gloss!

From tall towering pines to the tiniest sprout,
The woodland whispers bring joy all about.
With a giggle, a jiggle, all creatures unite,
In this land of laughter, all feels just right.

Echoes in the Canopy

Up high where the branches sway and creak,
Monkeys trade stories with apples to speak.
In playful competition, they whirl and spin,
While a parrot squawks, "This is how we begin!"

The squirrels made hats from the nattiest twigs,
Telling tall tales of the daintiest digs.
With acorns for buttons and smiles so wide,
They fashion a show, with critters as the guide.

A fox interrupts with a spicy new joke,
Chasing shadows and laughter, spreading the smoke.
The woodland erupts in a chorus of giggles,
As fireflies flutter and do playful wiggles.

In the heart of this wild and whimsical spree,
The echoes of joy float so carefree.
Amongst beams of sunlight, our stories entwine,
Crafted with laughter, timeless and fine.

Lore of the Lush Labyrinth

In the maze of leaves, a frog wears a hat,
Chasing after shadows and a chubby cat.
Squirrels debate who's the nuttiest fool,
While wise old owls play chess by a pool.

Rabbits steal carrots, plan a grand feast,
Juggling the veggies, they dance like a beast.
Deer laugh at the raccoons' tangled attire,
As fireflies giggle, igniting desire.

Mice make a band, with cheese as their prize,
Singing sweet melodies, to everyone's surprise.
The wind whispers secrets, with a mischievous grin,
As the moon starts to chuckle, letting the fun begin.

And every corner turned, there's a tale to share,
Of the critters that roam, with silliness in the air.
Adventures unfold in this playful delight,
Where laughter and magic dance through the night.

Songs of the Soothing Stream

A fish with a banjo plucks tunes through the spray,
Dancing with minnows, they frolic and play.
Lily pads wobble with giggles and glee,
While turtles do backflips, as happy as can be.

Dragonflies buzz in a caffeinated spree,
Spinning their tales with a splash of esprit.
The water's a stage for the wildest of shows,
As frogs join the chorus, singing high and low.

Beetles in bowties tap dance on wet stones,
While catfish roll laughing and tossing their bones.
Crickets compose symphonies under the stars,
Cheering along with a chorus of bizarre.

The stream flows along, with tunes in its wake,
Every ripple and splash, a story to make.
In this merry orchestra of water and mirth,
Each note is a treasure, a gem of the earth.

Echoes from the Emerald Understory

In shadows of emerald, a snail takes a leap,
Wobbling and wobbling, he gives a loud beep.
Mice hold a party with snacks piled up high,
Frog croaks a toast, to the stars in the sky.

Woodpeckers hammer out tunes on a tree,
While ants play percussion with all of their spree.
A hedgehog in glasses reads tales of the brave,
As mushrooms stand guard, looking quite grave.

The gossiping trees swap their silliest whims,
Muffling their laughter through bright, leafy limbs.
With jokes and with jests that baffle the mind,
These echoes of laughter are one of a kind.

A beetle in sneakers sprints around the floor,
Chasing a shadow until he's no more.
In this world below, where whimsy is king,
The stories that thrive make the forest sing.

Portraits of the Pine-Protected Path

At the edge of the trail, a fox poses grand,
Adjusting his bow tie with a fancy hand.
He winks at a rabbit, who trips on a log,
While a turtle gives pointers, in a stuttery fog.

Bats paint sunsets with brushes of glee,
Creating wild portraits for all who can see.
A raccoon dons spectacles, scribbles with zest,
Arguing with squirrels on who's dressed the best.

Pine trees gossip and gossip some more,
About the last bear who tried to explore.
They chuckle and giggle, rustling each bough,
At the antics of creatures, both silly and sour.

Paths paved in laughter, with each weary tread,
Where legends unfold, and all worries are shed.
So wander the woods, let humor be your guide,
In this world of portraits where joy's amplified.

Mysteries in the Mossy Depths

In shadows deep where critters creep,
A squirrel plots his nutty heist,
With acorns stashed, his plans are hashed,
He dreams of snacks, and not of mice.

A frog in boots, he struts around,
While beetles dance in silly shoes,
A laugh erupts, they flip and bound,
While owls just hoot and share their views.

The mushrooms gossip, spores in flight,
They chuckle about a clumsy hare,
Who tripped on roots in sheer delight,
And rolled right through the forest fair.

With secrets tucked in leafy beds,
The forest giggles in the night,
As playful sprites weave dreams in threads,
They shimmer softly with delight.

Anecdotes from the Arborial Edge

Upon the edge where branches sway,
A raccoon juggles pinecone balls,
He drops one down with quite a play,
And all the forest giggles, calls.

The wise old owl gives head a shake,
As rabbits hop in silly lines,
They twirl and spin, for goodness' sake,
While teasing their fox friend with puns and signs.

A wallaby, quite out of breath,
Attempts a jump that's way too high,
He lands in bramble, quite a mess,
The forest sports a hearty sigh.

Each tree has tales, roots full of jest,
Their laughter echoes, fills the air,
In every nook, they find a quest,
As nature shares its jokes laid bare.

Chronicles of the Whispering Willows

Beneath the willows, whispers float,
A chipmunk tells of mishaps grand,
With tales of nuts that rock the boat,
And how she slipped into the sand.

The willows sway with knowing grins,
As fireflies blink and dance around,
A snail, with speed, tries to fit in,
When tumbleweeds all hit the ground.

A bashful bat joins in the fun,
He flips and flops, a comical sight,
A whirlwind of mischief has begun,
With laughter echoing through the night.

Now every whisper, every giggle,
Weaves stories rich like woven linen,
The willows hide their chuckles regal,
As twilight blues turn into grinning.

Nature's Enchanted Epics

In magical woods where creatures play,
A wily fox dons a cape so bright,
He struts the trails in a fancy way,
While frogs applaud with pure delight.

A hedgehog with a tiny hat,
Waddles by with utmost flair,
He tips it low, just fancy that,
As butterflies all stop and stare.

The trees hold court, and laughter swells,
With stories shared in leafy clumps,
Of clumsy bears and bustling bells,
As everyone's heart jumps and thumps.

Each epic tale, a playful jest,
In nature's arms, we dance and cheer,
The world's a stage, and all are guests,
Where joy awaits, and fun draws near.

Murmurs from the Mossy Floor

In shadows deep where whispers grow,
A squirrel juggles acorns, oh what a show!
The mushrooms giggle at his clumsy feet,
While the old tree chuckles, can't help but repeat.

A rabbit in a waistcoat, sips his tea,
Says, "Did you hear? The owl has a PhD!"
The frogs croak jokes beneath the moon's light,
While fireflies dance, much to their delight.

A hedgehog plays poker with a sly old fox,
Each bluff revealed by a rustling box.
The bats drop in, bring tales from the skies,
And the laughing leaves join in with their sighs.

They plot to have fun till the break of dawn,
With stories unending, the night barely gone.
So if you listen closely, you might just hear,
The happy tales from the forest we revere.

The Herbaceous Chronicles

Once stood a herb who dreamed to be bold,
To tell tales of mishaps and make fortunes untold.
But thyme got distracted by a flirtatious bee,
And sage told puns that made all plants pee.

At sunrise, they gathered, the mint and the chive,
Discussing their dreams of a herb-themed jive.
The basil just laughed, said, "You're all so strange!"
"Let's shake off the soil and give life a change."

The radish proposed, "Let's start a big band!"
With parsley on drums, and dill on demand.
But every time they played, the ground shook with glee,
As carrots did the twist, and the peas swung so free.

Lettuce took charge, a true veggie queen,
Said, "This is the silliest party I've seen!"
So herbs shared their laughter under the sun,
In a merry jubilee, where all felt like fun.

Creatures of the Twilit Thicket

In a leafy abode where laughter abounds,
A raccoon spilled snacks all over the grounds.
With popcorn and berries strewn all around,
The badger just giggled and played on the mound.

The hedgehogs held a dance to the croaks of a toad,
Twisting and turning on their little dirt road.
A porcupine trumpeted joy on a leaf,
While the owls exchanged tales better than belief!

Frogs jumped in with their slippery finesse,
Each hop a new story, a playful dress.
And the fireflies, lighting the night with their cheer,
Danced in a circle, bringing all creatures near.

But watch as they feasted on bug cake supreme,
With laughter erupting, it felt like a dream.
In the thicket of twilight, where fun never stops,
Creatures unite, with giggles and hops.

Nectar of the Narrative

Gather 'round, dear friends, let the stories begin,
With honey and laughter, we know we'll win.
A bumblebee poet buzzed through a rhyme,
While the wildflowers danced, all in sync, all in time.

A butterfly burst forth with humor afloat,
Saying, "Why did the caterpillar bring a coat?"
The crowd all erupted, from fern to the oak,
In this meadow of mirth, where all love to joke.

The ants wrote epics, their prose full of zest,
While the ladybugs critiqued like they were the best.
There stood a tall sunflower, bowing its head,
As it listened and giggled at tales being fed.

So take a sip of this nectar divine,
Where every word spun is perfectly fine.
For laughter and stories, bring joy without measure,
In this land of delight, be it humor or treasure.

Chronicles of the Hidden Hollow

In a hollow where squirrels hold court,
Every acorn's a prize, oh what a sport!
The rabbits debate over peppermint leaves,
While wise old owls pretend to believe.

Beneath branches, the mischief runs rife,
With chipmunks spinning tales of their life.
The fox, ever sly, plays the jester's role,
Crafting jokes that make trees laugh and console.

A raccoon, with dreams of a grand dinner feast,\nHunts
for lost treasures, the greatest of beasts.
Yet each shiny object turns out to be
Just a bottle cap from some human's spree.

So, gather round friends, let's laugh and cheer,
In this hollow of secrets, no room for fear.
With giggles and grins, we'll dance with glee,
In a world where jokes grow like flowers on a tree.

Legends of the Leafy Bastion

In the leafy bastion, a deer sings out loud,
While a bear in a tutu prances, so proud.
The hedgehogs hold wrestling matches at night,
They claim it's the best form of exercise, right?

The frogs in their jackets hop joyfully high,
Gossiping tales of a passing sky guy.
They crack up at wolves who can't howl straight,
Turns out even the fiercest can sometimes be late.

The trees have a riddle that no one can solve,
Every creature baffled, trying to evolve.
But the skunk just shrugs, with a wink in his eye,
He's learned that the punchlines are where fun will lie!

So gather your laughter, bring zest to the scene,
In the bastion of leaves, the air's always green.
Where every adventure is spun with delight,
And legends keep tumbling, through day and through night.

Murmurs of the Mysterious Thicket

In the thicket, whispers dance on the breeze,
Where the butterflies chat with the buzzing bees.
The shadows weave tales of a squirrel on stilts,
Who performs for the critters, enacting their wilts.

A grumpy old crow caws a grumpy old rhyme,
But the rabbits just chuckle, they know it's his time.
For even the grumpiest birds must admit,
Laughter is sweeter than any old wit.

The hedges hold secrets of giggles and glee,
Of dragons made tiny by magic, you see?
They fly with the fairies, they slide down the stream,
Creating a world where all critters can dream.

So wander the thicket, where murmurs abound,
With joy tucked away, in each nook to be found.
Where every twig snap leads to a funny parade,
And the stories of laughter never ever fade.

The Storyteller's Trail

On the trail where the fables weave and spin,
A turtle spins yarns, with a goofy grin.
The paths hold riddles sung loud by the thrush,
While the ants tap dance in a curious rush.

With each twist and turn, a new tale unfolds,
Of cats in top hats and brave knightly squirrels.
The path is alive with a giggling sound,
Mixing surprise with the wonders all around.

A magic old willow tells tales from the past,
Of friendships and laughter that forever last.
But behind the stout trunk, a fox had a plan,
To turn all those stories to schemes he began.

So follow the trail where the laughter runs free,
Where every old story can become a glee.
For the storytellers are waiting, that's true,
To share every quirk that makes mirth bloom anew.

Murmurs of Mischief in the Meadow

In a field where whispers play,
A rabbit danced, then lost his way.
He tripped on grass and gave a squeak,
The butterflies laughed, oh so unique.

A hedgehog wore a pointy hat,
While squirrels gossiped, cheeky and fat.
They spun tall tales of leafy dread,
As wise old owls just shook their head.

The daisies giggled in the breeze,
A quirk of nature, quite the tease.
They twirled and swayed with every jest,
Encouraging lemmings to join the quest.

So hear the whispers in the grass,
Where every critter's got some sass.
In this land of leafy cheer,
Mischief blooms throughout the year.

Chronicles of the Cunning Creatures

A fox in shades, so sly and spry,
Played chess with crows that swooped and fly.
They squawked and honked, each move a jest,
The board was made of twigs—what a fest!

The raccoon stole the scene, it's true,
Swapping shiny goods, he'd trade for stew.
With pie tin hats and forks for swords,
He led a charge of mischievous hordes.

A badger found a stinky sock,
Screamed, "I've found the treasure's rock!"
But when he dug, what a surprise:
Just moldy fruit and insect pies!

This tale rolls on through whispers bright,
A creature's jest, a neighboring fight.
With laughs and roars from every tree,
Those cunning beings, wild and free.

Legends of the Luminous Leaf

Once glowed a leaf from trees of green,
With sparkles bright, a wondrous scene.
The bugs would dance and take a spin,
"Oh look!" they'd say, "The party's in!"

A beetle with a top hat fine,
Rapped on the bark, his voice divine.
With jokes and rhymes, he stole the show,
While ladybugs hummed to and fro.

Fireflies flickered, nimble and light,
They painted stars in the velvet night.
The luminous leaf shone oh so grand,
While frogs croaked tunes across the land.

But one bright morn, the leaf took flight,
In search of fun, oh what a sight!
So gather round and take a peek,
For legends spread where creatures speak.

Secrets Under the Silvery Skies

Beneath the stars, a secret's spun,
Where whispers linger, and laughs are fun.
A raccoon thieved a silver spoon,
Danced with the moon, a nightly tune.

A squirrel crafted a tale so tall,
Of acorn treasure and autumn's ball.
With giggles ringing under bright beams,
They spun their story, weaving dreams.

A family of owls played hide and seek,
But sleepy eyes made them all weak.
As laughter echoed, a soft bat flew,
"I heard your secret, ah, I just blew!"

With each twinkling light in the sky above,
The creatures shared tales of laughter and love.
So venture forth, let the moonlight guide,
To secrets known where joy does abide.

The Lore of the Lush Expanse

In the thicket of whimsy, the rabbits conspire,
They wear tiny hats, and sip frothy choir.
With a wink and a nod, they host a grand feast,
Inviting all critters, from west to the east.

The squirrels juggle acorns, a nutty display,
While the fox in a tux tries to dance the ballet.
The owls spin tales, their wisdom on point,
But trip on their wings, what a comical joint!

Beneath leafy canopies, laughter takes flight,
With bad jokes performed by the toads every night.
They open their mouths, but the punchlines go flat,
Leaving everyone laughing, save one grumpy cat.

In the heart of this grove, the gnomes take a break,
With a wink and a chuckle, they bake a grand cake.
Yet each slice's a riddle, pranks tucked in deep,
Best consume it with caution, or lose track of sleep!

Parables of the Pine

In a grove of tall pines, the frogs tell a tale,
Of a prince in a puddle, who tried to set sail.
With a lily for a boat, he paddled in vain,
A soggy affair, yet he laughed in the rain.

The woodpecker drums out a beat on the trunk,
While the hedgehogs try dancing, but mostly just thunk.
They twirl and they wiggle, then roll in a pile,
With laughter all around, it's pure woodland style.

As the sun starts to set, the stories grow tall,
Of a brave little mouse who just thought he was small.
He climbed on a beetle, shouted, "I'm king!",
So the ants held a contest, a royal spring fling.

Now the creatures all gather, for fun and delight,
Sharing tales of the hero who danced through the night.
With a twinkle in their eyes and giggles galore,
In this bustling pine patch, who could ask for more?

Sagas from the Undergrowth

In the depths of the bushes, where mischief does thrive,
The snails throw a party; they're barely alive!
With a slide down a leaf, they giggle and cheer,
While the tortoise groans, "I'll just stick with my beer."

A wise old chameleon, with colors so bright,
Tells tales of his travels, from morning till night.
He changes his hue, practicing flair,
But the ants roll their eyes; he's a bit of a bear!

Mice wheel in a circle, on tiny toy cars,
While the owl at the end judges "Who'll reach the stars?"

A race full of hiccups, they crash and they roll,
Yet the laughter persists, as they all share the goal.

Through fables and giggles, the forest comes alive,
With riddles and pranks, oh, how they all thrive!
A patchwork of stories beneath old twisting roots,
Where the laughter of creatures has given them fruits.

Whimsy Among the Willows

In the shade of the willows, the badgers convene,
To plot silly capers, their mischief unseen.
With bows and balloon hats, they start a parade,
Their dance moves are clumsy, but no plans are laid.

The squirrels compete for the best acorn crown,
While the cardinals judge with a smile, not a frown.
Amid giggles and chatter, they create quite a scene,
In the sleepy old glade, where nonsense is keen.

The wind carries whispers of jokes from the reeds,
With the frogs spouting punchlines like colorful seeds.
But the turtles just chuckle, so slow in their way,
Saying, "Who needs to hurry when fun's here to stay?"

As the sun starts to dip, the shadows grow tall,
The critters gather 'round for a merry night call.
With stories of whimsy and laughter that bloomed,
In this kingdom of willows, joy is well-zoomed!

Reveries of the Rustling Leaves

Once in a grove, a squirrel wore shoes,
He danced with the breeze, spreading silly news.
The acorns would giggle, rolling in glee,
As branchy comedians performed a decree.

A fox donned a wig, thinking it suave,
He pranced by the brook, feeling quite brave.
The ducks clucked in chorus, giving a cheer,
While rabbits played cards, chugging root beer.

The trees shook their heads, laughing in time,
As crickets recited their best pudding rhyme.
The mushrooms chuckled, with tiny hats,
While the owls just hooted, enjoying the spats.

From sunup to dusk, their antics did sing,
Where laughter was currency, happiness king.
In this whimsied retreat, with giggles galore,
Each leaf held a secret, each root had a lore.

Tales of the Twilight Thicket

In the twilight thicket, where shadows collide,
A raccoon played poker, with kings at his side.
The badgers were bluffing, while critters could peek,
And the hedgehogs rolled dice, with squeaks and some squeaks.

The owl, who was wise, wore glasses too big,
While the beetles did breakdance, with moves that were swig.
A party of frogs kept the rhythm alive,
With croaks that turned tunes into sweet jive.

The moon shone bright, like a disco ball high,
As fireflies twinkled, like stars in the sky.
With snacks made of berries and drinks warm and sweet,
They feasted and laughed, as they moved to the beat.

And with each passing hour, their joy became thick,
They shared all their stories, each laugh was a trick.
In the twilight thicket, what fun they would weave,
Forever reminding, there's joy to believe.

The Enchanted Elm's Lament

Under the elm, with branches so wide,
A gnome took a nap, with a mushroom for a guide.
His dreams filled with jellybeans swirling around,
While the ladybugs giggled, without making a sound.

A turtle in boots, so proud of his style,
Waddled through paths, taking time for a smile.
He chased after butterflies, laughing in flight,
While the ants shouted jokes, causing quite a delight.

The breeze carried whispers of secrets and fun,
As the chipmunks played tag, from sun until sun.
A dance party started, with a twig as a pole,
And the elm stood there grumbling, but deep down, felt whole.

Though roots felt the weight of all jokes that were told,
The laughter of friends kept their spirits quite bold.
In that enchanting realm, where fables are spun,
The elm learned, joy comes with each crazy pun.

Whispers of the Wandering Wind

The wandering wind had quite stories to share,
Of a hedgehog named Oliver, who lost all his hair.
He wore on his back a bright patchwork quilt,
Claiming it made him a creature of guilt.

Through valleys and hills, the whispers would flutter,
As the otters performed, doing tricks in the butter.
The frogs let out croaks that echoed with flair,
Turning mud into dance floors, without a care.

With every cheeky breeze, a new tale would sprout,
Of tricky raccoons, and their schemes all about.
A family of owls debated their names,
Each suggestion brought laughter, igniting new flames.

So listen real close, let the wind be your guide,
With giggles and tales that swirl far and wide.
In this merry mix of shenanigans bright,
Joy hides in the whispers—so take wing, take flight!

The Tapestry of Twisting Vines

In a tangle of green, a parrot sings,
Telling tales of silly things.
A squirrel dressed up in a suit so fine,
Declares he's off to dine on pine.

A turtle on roller skates whirls around,
While rabbits wear hats and leap off the ground.
The laughter of leaves rustles away,
As the woodpeckers join in the play.

A fox slipped on acorns, what a sight,
He waved in a panic, tried to take flight.
But ended up laughing with all of his pals,
In a riot of giggles beneath waving gales.

The vines gently sway, weaving fun in the air,
As the critters all gather, with laughter to share.
Each twist in the tale, each turn in the day,
Is stitched into yarns that frolic and play.

The Glimmering Glen's Sagas

In a glen where the sunbeams dance with glee,
A rabbit juggles carrots — quite the sight to see!
The hedgehog spins tales of jams and pies,
With a wink from his eye and laughter that flies.

A wise old owl wears spectacles on his beak,
Reciting the fables of furry and sleek.
The dew on the grass shines like little stars,
As the mice clap their paws and shout, "Huzzah!"

A dancing brook babbles in silly tones,
While frogs tap their feet on sticky stones.
The fireflies twinkle, wearing glowworm hats,
As the story unfolds, how the giggles amass!

With every tall tale, the glen comes alive,
Where humor and joy joyously thrive.
A place filled with whimsy, no worries in sight,
As laughter resounds until the fall of night.

Starlight Stories in the Underbrush

Under the stars, where shadows play hide,
A raccoon with dreams takes his friends for a ride.
They hop on a toad and go for a spin,
Squealing with laughter as the magic begins.

A chipmunk recites, with flair on the stage,
Tales of a bear who raved like a sage.
He danced with the daisies, oh what a sight!
While the night creatures giggled in pure delight.

A party of owls, with cookies and cream,
Munching on treats and living the dream.
As the night deepens, the stories come alive,
Under the twinkling mosaic where whimsy will thrive.

With a whisk and a swish, more stories unfold,
Chasing away worries with laughter so bold.
In the underbrush, where dreams take a flight,
The critters unite to share joy through the night.

The Magical Canopy's Tales

Up high in the branches, where the breezes blend,
A monkey spins tales that twist and bend.
He swings with his pals, all merrily grinning,
As the laughter erupts, it's a game they are winning.

A parrot drops in, a grandiose flair,
Reciting wild fables while twirling in air.
The sloths hang around, all slow and serene,
Making comments so wise, they could rival a queen.

The canopy shimmers with giggles and cheer,
As the antics grow wilder with every leap near.
A worm in a bowtie charms the whole crew,
With tales that are silly, yet somehow seem true.

Every branch is a stage; each leaf wears a grin,
As the magical canopy welcomes them in.
With stories of laughter and fun in the mix,
The woods all abound with their own brand of tricks.

Chronicles of the Sylvan Realm

In a land where the squirrels dance,
The rabbits hold a grand old prance.
They tiptoe 'round the tall oak trees,
Hoping to tease the buzzing bees.

The wise old owl gives a hoot,
For he's found a lost, silly boot.
It belonged to a mouse named Lou,
Who wore it just to feel brand new.

The hedgehogs roll in happy glee,
As they play a game of hide and seek.
But careful now, don't ruffle a leaf,
Or you'll scare away the mischievous chief!

And when the sun begins to dip,
The fireflies gather for a trip.
They light the way for all to see,
In this quirky realm, oh so free.

Echoes of the Ancient Trees

Beneath branches where whispers hide,
The raccoons gossip, cheeks puffed wide.
They trade tales of the berry feast,
While the elder tree laughs, quite the beast.

A fox in socks prances around,
Declaring he's the fastest in town.
His paws, though small, defy the odds,
Proving that fun beats all the gods.

The wise crickets chirp a tune,
As fluffy clouds drift like a balloon.
They sing of dreams, both big and small,
In the shade of the great tree wall.

When evening comes, they gather tight,
Playing games till the stars feel bright.
In the echoes, laughter sings,
Capturing joy that the forest brings.

The Fauna's Folktale

Once a turtle raced a playful hare,
But the hare just napped without a care.
When he awoke, the finish line neared,\nThe turtle's cheer soon calmed his weird.

With winks and nods, the birds all chimed,
As the hedgehog recited what he'd rhymed.
Across the burrows, trading some tales,
Of blundering foxes and harebrained snails.

The rabbits built a rocket ship,
With dreams of snacks on a cosmic trip.
They laughed and flailed, quite out of sync,
With carrots packed, they'd not miss a shrink.

Underneath the moon's soft glow,
Dancing shadows steal the show.
With a raucous laugh and a friendly call,
Friends unite, and together they sprawl.

Shadows of the Moonlit Grove

In the shadows where moonbeams play,
The owls tell jokes in a quirky way.
A raccoon, dressed in a tiny vest,
Claims he's the king; oh, what a jest!

A bat swoops down, wearing a cape,
Declaring he's crafted a grand escape.
But tangled in branches, he starts to whine,
"Oh, where's my dinner? Was it divine?"

The frogs croak loudly, forming a band,
Beating their drums made from matted sand.
With each ribbit, they burst into song,
In this strange grove where all belong.

As night deepens and friends all meet,
The laughter echoes, oh so sweet.
In shadows' arms, they find their place,
Sharing stories with joy and grace.

www.ingramcontent.com/pod-product-compliance
Lightning Source LLC
Chambersburg PA
CBHW071854160426
43209CB00003B/552